To-

Fro.
Cynthia
Humphries

OTHER BOOKS IN THE TO-GIVE-AND-TO-KEEP® SERIES:

Welcome to the New Baby
To a very special Daughter
To a very special Grandmother
To a very special Grandpa
Happy Anniversary
To my very special Love
To a very special Mother
To a very special Son
To a very special Grandson

To a very special Dad
To a very special Friend
To a very special Granddaughter
Wishing you Happiness
To my very special Husband
Merry Christmas
To a very special Sister
To my very special Wife
To my very special Teacher

Published simultaneously in 1996 by Exley Giftbooks in the USA and
Exley Publications Ltd in Great Britain.

12 11 10 9

Copyright © Helen Exley 1996
The moral right of the author has been asserted

ISBN 1-86187-366-2

Edited by Helen Exley.
Printed in China.

Exley Publications Ltd, 16 Chalk Hill, Watford, Herts WD19 4BG, UK.
Exley Publications LLC, 185 Main Street, Spencer, MA 01562, USA
www.helenexleygiftbooks.com

Acknowledgements: The publishers are grateful for permission to reproduce copyright
material. While every effort has been made to trace copyright holders, Exley
Publications would be pleased to hear from any not here acknowledged: Ogden Nash:
The extracts "Love is to need...." and "An occasional lucky guess....", and the extract
from "Marriage Lines" are reprinted by permission of the publisher Little, Brown & Co
and Curtis Brown; Pam Brown, Charlotte Gray and Jenny de Vries: published with
permission © Helen Exley 1996.

To a special couple
on your
WEDDING DAY

A HELEN EXLEY GIFTBOOK
ILLUSTRATIONS BY JULIETTE CLARKE

The greatest gift that I would wish
for you is empathy, the skill to
see into each other's minds and
hearts with love and
understanding, and to help each
other to realize your dreams.

EXLEY

A NEW LIFE

In the opinion of the world,
marriage ends all, as it does in a
comedy. The truth is precisely the
opposite: it begins all.

ANNE SOPHIE SWETCHINE

...

Marriage is a serious business, but
love turns the grey of life to gold.

MIRIAM OSBORNE

...

Marriage is the place where you
can at last be comfortable.
You can take off the too-tight
shoes and dress for comfort.

PAM BROWN, b.1928

...

A marriage makes of two fractional lines a whole; it gives to two purposeless lives a work, and doubles the strength of each to perform it; it gives to two questioning natures a reason for living, and something to live for.

MARK TWAIN (1835-1910)

…

That quiet mutual gaze of a trusting husband and wife is like the first moment of rest or refuge from a great weariness or a great danger.

GEORGE ELIOT (MARY ANN EVANS) (1819-1880)

…

Marriage sets mathematics on its head – for at one swoop it halves all troubles. Being shared, multiplies joys out of all reckoning, divides responsibilities, doubles perception.

PAM BROWN, b.1928

…

<u>TO YOUR HAPPY MARRIAGE!</u>

There is a certain ease in a happy marriage – a
certainty, a contentment, that lies beneath all
change. May the coming years bring you ever
closer. May they give you contentment and
adventure, astonishments and peace.

PAM BROWN, b.1928

. . .

[May] this marriage be wine with halvah, honey dissolving in milk.

This marriage be the leaves and fruit of a date tree.

This marriage be women laughing together for days on end.

This marriage a sign for us to study.

This marriage, beauty.

This marriage, a moon in a light-blue sky.

This marriage, this silence fully mixed with spirit.

RUMI, WRITTEN FOR HIS SON'S WEDDING

…

May heaven grant you in all things your heart's desire – husband, house and a happy peaceful home. For there is nothing better in this world than that a man and woman, sharing the same ideas, keep house together. It discomforts their enemies and makes the hearts of their friends glad – but they themselves know more about it than anyone.

HOMER (8TH CENTURY B.C.), FROM "THE ODYSSEY"

MY PROMISE TO YOU ...

I add my breath to your breath

That our days may be long in the earth

That the days of our people may be long

That we may be one person

That we may finish our roads together

KERES INDIAN SONG

...

Whither thou goest, I will go; and where thou

lodgest, I will lodge; thy people shall be my

people, and thy God my God.

RUTH 1:16

...

Come live with me, and be my love,

And we will some new pleasures prove

Of golden sands, and crystal brooks,

With silken lines, and silver hooks.

JOHN DONNE (1572-1631), FROM "THE BAIT"

...

Romance

I will make you brooches and toys for your delight
Of bird-song at morning and star-shine at night
I will make a palace, fit for you and me,
Of green days in forests, and blue days at sea.

I will make my kitchen and you shall keep your room
Where white flows the river and bright blows the broom,
And you shall wash your linen and keep your body while
In rainfall at morning and dewfall at night.

And this shall be for music when no one else is near,
The fine song for singing, the rare song to hear!
That only I remember, that only you admire,
Of the broad road that stretches and the roadside fire.

ROBERT LOUIS STEVENSON (1850-1894)

WEDDING DAY!

I don't think I had any concerns when I was
walking down the aisle. I was very happy. It's the
culmination of everyone's dream to find a person
you can love who loves you.

TIPPER GORE

...

Where would we be without weddings? They flower
in the bleakest landscape – gifts of hope and
courage, faith and love, in a weary world.

CHARLOTTE GRAY, b.1937

...

May this day be perfect
– or as near as dammit so!
Don't worry if the bridal wreathe settles at a
slightly jaunty angle,
or a wisp of hair escapes it.
Don't worry if the car gets stuck in traffic
and the vicar seems to have a nasty cold.
Don't worry if the organ wheezes
and the pageboy wriggles
and the Best Man fumbles with the ring.
You see each other –
and all else blurs away to insignificance.
Later – you will remember,
and laugh together.
But now no triviality can penetrate.
Love transforms everything.
Even Aunt Mildred's hat.

PAM BROWN, b.1928

...

... I love thee with the breath,

Smiles, tears, of all my life! –

ELIZABETH BARRETT BROWNING (1806-1861)

...

Now we will feel no rain

for each of us will be shelter for the other.

Now we will feel no cold

for each of us will be warmth for the other.

Now there is no more loneliness

for each of us will be companion to the other.

There is only one life before us

and our seasons will be long and good.

FROM AN APACHE WEDDING BLESSING

It's all I have to bring to-day,

This, and my heart beside,

This, and my heart, and all the fields,

And all the meadows wide.

Be sure you count, should I forget, –

Some one the sun could tell, –

This, and my heart, and all the bees

Which in the clover dwell.

EMILY DICKINSON (1830-1886)

…

Love me with thine hand stretched out

Freely – open-minded.

ELIZABETH BARRETT BROWNING (1806-1861)

ONLY LOVE

Falling in love is largely delusion – two hearts

translating reality to dream.

But love is reality itself – accepting, cherishing,

delighting in the individual oddities

that make a man and woman

what they are.

PAM BROWN, b.1928

To love is nothing. To be loved is something.
To love, and be loved, is everything.

T. TOLIS V.

…

Love alone is capable of uniting living beings in
such a way as to complete and fulfil them, for it
alone takes them and joins them by what is deepest
in themselves.

PIERRE TEILHARD DE CHARDIN (1881-1955)

…

Love is like a mine. You go deeper and deeper.
There are passages, caves, whole strata. You
discover entire geological eras.

CHRISTOPHER ISHERWOOD

…

Nothing in life is as good as the marriage of true
minds between man and woman. As good?
It is life itself.

PEARL BUCK (1892-1973)

The keystone to any marriage is one word:

"WE".

PAM BROWN, b.1928

...

Love, the magician, knows this little trick
whereby two people walk in different
directions yet always remain side by side.

HUGH PRATHER

...

The entire sum of existence is the magic of
being needed by just one person.

V. PUTNAM

...

It takes a lot of courage to show your
dreams to someone else.

ERMA BOMBECK, b.1927

...

There shall be such a oneness between
you that when one weeps, the other
shall taste salt.

PROVERB

...

Love is that condition in which the
happiness of another person is essential
to your own.

ROBERT HEINLEIN

...

HANDLE WITH GREAT CARE

A marriage where not only esteem, but passion is
kept awake, is, I am convinced, the most perfect
state of sublunary happiness: but it requires great
care to keep this tender plant alive.

FRANCES BROOKE

...

I would like to have engraved inside every wedding
band, "Be kind to one another." This is the Golden
Rule of marriage and the secret of making love last
through the years.

RANDOLPH RAY

...

Every enduring marriage involves an unconditional
commitment to an imperfect person.

GARY SMALLEY, FROM "LOVE IS A DECISION"

...

In the consciousness of belonging together, in the
sense of constancy, resides the sanctity, the beauty
of matrimony, which helps us to endure pain more
easily, to enjoy happiness doubly, and to give rise to
the fullest and finest development of our nature.

FANNY LEWALD (1811-1889)

...

Love is to need, and needing, to be needed.
It is the patient architect that builds
Misunderstandings into understanding;
The sunrise, and the waking sea it gilds;
The far new shore, and the precarious landing.

OGDEN NASH (1902-1971)

...

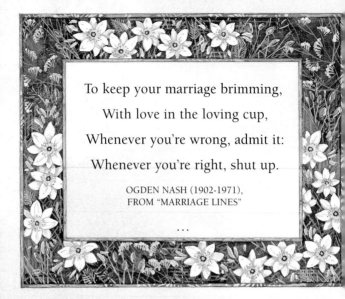

To keep your marriage brimming,

With love in the loving cup,

Whenever you're wrong, admit it:

Whenever you're right, shut up.

OGDEN NASH (1902-1971),
FROM "MARRIAGE LINES"

...

THOSE UPS AND DOWNS

An occasional lucky guess as to what makes a wife
tick is the best a man can hope for. Even then, no
sooner has he learned how to cope with the tick
than she tocks.

OGDEN NASH (1902-1971)

...

Now some people think it's jolly for to lead

a single life,

But I believe in marriage and the

comforts of a wife.

In fact you might have quarrels, just an odd one

now and then,

It's worth your while a-falling out to

make it up again.

ENGLISH FOLK SONG

...

The great secret of a successful marriage is to treat

all disasters as incidents and none of the incidents

as disasters.

HAROLD NICHOLSON

...

A happy marriage is the union of two good

forgivers.

RUTH BELL GRAHAM

...

UNITED

You can never be happily married to another until you get a divorce from yourself. Successful marriage demands a certain death to self.

JERRY MCCANT

...

No strong marriage can be founded on "We'll see how long we can make it last," only on "We will make it last."

JENNY DE VRIES

...

"Spiritual surrender" is intentional. It is the result of the free and unencumbered use of one's will.

GERALD G. MAY

...

In loving one another you will discover not only the depth and breadth and height of each other's being – but your own.

PAM BROWN, b.1928

...

Two persons who have chosen each other out of all the species, with the design to be each other's mutual comfort and entertainment, have, in that action, bound themselves to be good-humoured, affable, discreet, forgiving, patient, and joyful, with respect to each other's frailties and perfections, to the end of their lives.

JOSEPH ADDISON (1672-1719)

...

None can be eternally united who have not died for each other.

COVENTRY PATMORE (1823-1896),
FROM "THE RED, THE ROOT AND THE FLOWER"

...

FOREVER TOGETHER

Treasure the love you receive above all.
It will survive long after your gold and good
health have vanished.

OG MANDINO

...

... Love bears all things, believes all things,
hopes all things, endures all things. Love
never ends....

I CORINTHIANS 13:4-8

...

A happy marriage is a long conversation that
always seems too short.

ANDRE MAUROIS (1885-1967)

...

Therefore mercifully ordain that we may become
aged together.

FROM "THE BOOK OF TOBIT"

...

FOR LIFE

Here begin the astonishments!

For you have only just begun to

know each other.

May this be a journey of wonder, laughter,

sympathy and kind companionship.

JENNY DE VRIES

...

It is a lovely thing to have a husband and a wife developing together and having the feeling of falling in love again. That is what marriage really means. Helping one another to reach the full status of being persons, responsible and autonomous beings who do not run away from life.

PAUL TOURNIER (1898-1986)

...

I think a man and a woman should choose each other for life, for the simple reason that a long life with all its accidents is barely enough for a man and a woman to understand each other; and in this case to understand is to love.

JOHN BUTLER YEATS (1865-1939)

...

Take hands – look into each other's eyes. Each year you ill discover more of one another – and love more deeply.

PAM BROWN, b.1928

...